Chaos

Adam Nevarez

Dead by Daybreak
Fresno, Ca

All Rights Reserved

Text and Photographs
Copyright Adam Nevarez ©2022

ISBN: 978-1-9524671-2-7
Published July 2022

Production Assistance provided by HBE Publishing

All rights reserved. No part of this book may be used or reproduced in any manner whatsoever without written permission from the publisher, except in the case of brief quotations embodied in critical articles or reviews.

Dead by Daybreak

Fresno, Ca

Contents

Djarum Black And 805	2
Beautiful Stranger	4
The Beginning	6
Brothers	8
All the Difference	10
Full	12
Roulette	14
Possibility	16
Fragile	18
I.A.L	22
Threnody	24
For Jared (Too Early)	26
Curiosity	28
Gravity	30
Incurable	32
F2.8	34
Cigarette Perch	36
Farewell (Bootcamp)	38
The Captive	40
Sick Of You	42

chaos

Djarum Black And 805

I have no choices begging question
- no regret of either kind.
A drunken kiss will surely destine
friendship to be left behind.
It seems the distance made us strangers
- we fell to lust at first sight.
But morning was painfully sober
when you crawled back to the light.

chaos

Beautiful Stranger

I think of our time together
as a book I could not finish.
For all these questions without answer
(which cannot end a final chapter)
have left my mind with this one wish:
you were still a beautiful stranger.

The Beginning

This bond will break, it cannot bend.
Hold fast- I cannot stop
the beginning of our end.

Who is to blame? We both had doubt.
But voiceless fear is an open wound
and silent answers sold us out,

You are not dead to me, my dear
- yet if I feel no life with you
then you're the death of me I fear.

But I became your every breath!
So can I truly call it living
if I leave you to certain death?

Blood is pouring from the suture.
These broken hearts we stitched together
bleed and stain our every future.

Who is to blame? We both knew change.
The children we were died in our arms
- the face in the mirror was strange.

This bond will break, so leave it be.
It was made for a different life
and from that life we now are free.

chaos

Brothers

Neither one of us is who we were
that night you swore you'd stay the same.
Of brotherhood's bond we could be sure,
but separate paths brought separate pain.

All the Difference

Crawling, slipping, scrambling
through a forest of memories.
A fierce and frantic searching
for a path I should have taken.

Full

There's no feeling quite as hollow
- no regret quite so sad
- as knowing that I could have changed
and wishing that I had.

chaos

Roulette

It was a moment a too late
but that's all it would take.
I saw my chance, I took the gamble
- I ignored the odds of survival.
You always knew the stakes.

It was a moment too late
but that's all it would take.
You pressed your body tight against me,
rejecting our reality.
I knew your will would break.

It was a moment too late,
our lips found each other.
Words we swore would stay unspoken
laid bare our twisted passion
- you loaded the revolver.

I thought I knew how this woud end
when I pulled the fucking trigger.
Every lie that brought you closer
was a bullet in the chamber
- I kept spinning the cylinder.

I thought I knew how this would end
because this wasn't my first game.
But the lust that burned in your eyes
- that willingness to cut all ties
- warned me that your score stood the same.

I should have known how this would end
because I knew what you had done.
You dug six feet and bid farewell
- one last muzzle flash broke the spell
- he's buried with the smoking gun.

I should have known how this would end
when I pulled the fucking trigger.
But I lost count of all my lies
- we were both too drunk to realize
it was not an empty chamber.

Possibility

It was so many years ago
- a life time for one as young as me.
Every day the wonder grows:
was love a possibility?

Fragile

From fragile innocence
to the first transgression,
a span without measure
seperates them forever.

chaos

I.A.L

Regret's most bitter pain
took hold of my sold heart
as I tried to refrain
from freeing this burning spark.

Threnody

Let tomorrow bring for me
a blood red sun's cloudless break.
For her light I will not see,
- to her light I will not wake.

I care not if chance or fate
- in sorrow have I wandered
and cursed Death for being so late.
This is the night I wanted.

Love and hope were all I knew:
every breath I would revere.
But love passed like morning dew
and hope fell to my worst fear.

Because our love was youthful,
there was nothing Time could do.
But Fate was very watchful,
and no bounds his great arm knew.

Thus for me the night had come
and all the world slept and dreamed.
But my visions then were from
opened eyes it would have seemed.

Through the darkness I held fast
to sanity till the dawn.
Only when I breathe my last
will these bleak visions be gone.

Now in this concluding hour
I exalt your memory.
In this I find the power
to accept eternity.

Let tomorrow bring for me
a blood red sun's cloudless break.
Death, tonight, will set me free,
then by my love will I wake.

When of my breath I am shorn
and you bear me to the ground,
sing no threnody forlorn!
Utter not a mournful sound.

Bear me not there with weeping
for I would you weep no tear.
Lay me beside my darling,
for my heart has rested here.

chaos

For Jared (Too Early)

Was it merely chance?
Oh let it not be destiny!
For am I to understand
that by will of divine hand
my heart is burdened with cruelty?

Is this punishment?
Then countless souls plead guilty!
For all the tears that my eyes pour
fall with the tears of hundreds more
for Death has come too early!

chaos

Curiosity

Our innocence was not stolen.
Our innocence was not lost.
It was the birthright gladly given
to stay hunger at any cost.
What a wretchedness it is to crave
all the fruit you never tasted.
Do you think this hunger you can stave
- was your father's wisdom wasted?

Gravity

Unconscious gravitation
towards depravity
plagues me with the question:
is immorality
the cause or consequence
of human nature?

chaos

Incurable

I see your flawless features
in stranger's faces.
Am I haunted or obsessed?

chaos

F2.8

Immortality was
an imperfect replication.
nothing more
than a lifeless imitation.

Cigarette Perch

Last song, last drink, oh won't you dance?
Not now? Not me? Don't let go,
darling we don't get a second chance.

chaos

Farewell (Bootcamp)

He gave me his only house key,
said, "Put it on the shelf."
I knew then for many years
I would laugh by myself.

The Captive

Shadows embrace this mournful hall
as the night beckons me.
In vain I seek her dreamy call
- I struggle endlessly.

No more is darkness a solace
that will shelter my restless mind.
I close my eyes, but I'm sleepless
- there is no comfort there to find.

I am plagued with lucid visions
of the shame I tried to bury.
These memories are like phantoms
- each bears the name "Depravity."

Can I forget what I have done
- find the strength to start anew?
Will I ever find redemption
- hope it is lasting and true?

What hope is there to press the fight
just to risk falling once again?
For should I wish to see the light
I run the risk of being human.

What can one do in such defeat
when this despair is hollowing
- knowing that there is no retreat
and remorse ever following?

Breathe the fear of damnation:
with terror one will suffocate.
Succumbing to the poison,
he falls in the balance of Fate.

So I surrender to the shadows
- my soul in captivity.
And I brace for the time to follow
- how can I be free of me?

Sick Of You

Her voice clamors through my thoughts:
the headache the morning after.
Sweet perfume still fills my nose,
but dare smell whiskey still hungover?